Sojourn Book Revi

MW00856824

"The next-best thing to actually taking your own sojourn would be reading this book. It will place you, mentally and emotionally, into your very own cabin in the woods, where life is leisurely, your schedule and pace are your own, and your surroundings are soul expanding."

- Ann Perry, Book Reviewer for The Norris Bulletin

"Meenach's book serves both as a guidebook and an example of how simple, yet spectacular a sojourn can be. With her open-ended options, the sky's the limit."

- Susan Larson, Columnist for the Gwinnett Daily News

Kathy Meenach's book, _Sojourns, Anyone?_, is personal storytelling at its finest. Written in a conversational voice and with an artist's eye of appreciation, this Guide to Rejuvenation takes you on an uplifting journey back to your very own spirit within.

- Sabra Bowers, Poet/Blogger/Writer, Atlanta, GA

"It feels like you don't even read *Sojourns, Anyone?* as Kathy literally takes you along her four day sojourn. From the pictures Kathy paints with her words, scrumptious foods she prepares, to the beautiful photographs she has taken with her 35mm camera. You are there. You can feel the heat of the fireplace, taste the wine and see the sunsets.

Kathy has provided resources, questions, recipes and ideas to help you figure out your sojourn. It's like having your own personal "Kathy's Sojourn Kit". I feel *Sojourns, Anyone?* is for women and men; as everyone needs time to relax, recharge, remember, rediscover and rejuvenate. You deserve a loving gift to yourself. Enjoy your experience of *Sojourns, Anyone?!*"

- Dawn McDonald, Fellow Sojourner, Atlanta, GA

FORWARD

Twelve years ago I embarked on a sojourn that changed my outlook on life. Even then, life was non-stop-go in every aspect and if anything, the world has stepped up the pace moving in Nano seconds!

As my journey moved forward I became single, my beautiful daughters grew up and I lost the most important man in my life, my daddy; which led to the question . . . what do I want at this time of my life?

I took a 5 year sojourn to San Diego, California. It was an amazing time of exploration, creating community and allowing me to be me. While I was there, my oldest daughter got married and started a family. This led my journey back to the East coast to be a part of their family. Oh what an adventure it was sojourning back, but I'll save that for another story.

I moved to Opelika, Alabama. While sitting on my porch in the spring of 2020, I re-read this book and felt the relevancy of sojourning and self-discovery. The world slowed down and gave us opportunity to be with our own thoughts, to learn what important things we want in our lives. Why not take those thoughts a little further by taking a sojourn when the time is right?

It's all here in my book, the steps to help you plan a sojourn to create yourself in this new shift that has become our life. Now is the perfect time to explore and research the possibilities.

I reach out to you with a re-print of my book. Extend your own journey and continue to discover you!

Kathy

Sojourns, Anyone?
A Guide to Rejuvenation

By Kathy Meenach

Sojourn: Stay or dwell in a place for a short period of time

Fernhead Publishing
www.fernheadpublishing.com

Second Printing Fernhead Publishing © 2020
Suwanee, Georgia, USA
First Printing Heron Lee Publication, Inc. © 2009
Book & Cover design: Apex Book Manufacturing, Inc.
Alpharetta, Georgia, USA

Photography by Kathy Meenach

Publisher's Cataloging-in-Publication Data
Meenach, Kathy.
Join Kathy on her sojourn and discover the possibilities of
taking your own sojourn. -1st ed.
    p.   cm.
ISBN: 978-0-9982199-3-6 (pbk)
ISBN: 978-0-9982199-4-3 (eBook)
1. Self-Help   2. Travel/Sojourn   3. Memoire   4. Cooking
158-dc23
Library of Congress Control Number: 2020912243

Printed in the United States of America

This book is dedicated to all women who aspire to find themselves.

Table of Contents

Introduction 11

Planning a Sojourn 13

What I Learned 17

Day One 19

Journal Entry One 23

Day Two 25

Journal Entry Two 31

Day Three 35

Journal Entry Three 51

Day Four 53

Journal Entry Four 57

Why Take a Sojourn? 59

Your Sojourn 61

Food For Thought 69

Introduction

Life as we know it in the United States seems to move at the speed of light. Every moment is filled with some type of project or chore. If you are a woman, life is one big multi-task. How many things can you do at once? You try to squeeze in all that you want to accomplish in a 24 hour day. Your brain is constantly segmenting, compartmentalizing or organizing.

When you finally stop at the end of a day, your body may give out but your brain finds it almost impossible to stop, making it difficult to fall asleep, to get the much needed rest you need to wake up the next day and start all over again. Does this sound like you? Have you chosen the role of complacency, doing the same thing day in and day out? Are you afraid to break out of this mode because it's just too comfortable? Are you feeling the weight of your responsibilities in trying to be the ultimate mother, the most supportive wife, always the best friend, the hardest worker in the office, be the cleanest housekeeper in the neighborhood, the perfect hostess, be the most extraordinary lover?

Sojourns, Anyone?

Yes, life should be lived, but you have a role in living it also. For the most part, women tend to be nurturing towards others, responsible, always putting other people ahead of their own needs. What about your responsibility to yourself? What have you done for yourself lately?

I'm married to a wonderful man, mother to two beautiful teenage daughters, slave to a chocolate Labrador Retriever, working full time and living in an ever evolving dream home nestled in the woods. My life is non-stop-go. The demands are overwhelming. By the end of the day, I am too tired to take time for myself and my limit has been reached!

I realized I needed time for myself and needed it badly! Why not take a trip, a sojourn, breaking the endless cycle and going somewhere quiet and peaceful with no demands or responsibilities monopolizing my time; just me . . . spending time with myself. In this book I've included journal entries, excerpts and photographs illustrating my journey to help bring you into the moment of my experience.

Planning a Sojourn

So, how to begin? You can either plan your sojourn or just pick up and go. My first sojourn destination requirements were a cabin with a fireplace in the mountains, remote but not too distant. I did extensive research on the internet and skimmed through some travel books looking at various places to stay. Finding an interesting place, I looked at the surrounding area to see if there were parks and hiking trails, quaint little towns or any events of interest at the time of my trip.

After selecting several options, I contacted the proprietors to find out the availability and best prices. Since February is considered offseason, there was a possibility of getting a price break. A website caught my eye for rental of a small cabin built in 1860 located in the mountains of Tennessee, The Cabin on Cedar Ridge. It was a one-room cabin with a kitchen, fireplace and a loft bedroom. There was a porch, with rockers, on the front of the cabin. The price was right; only a 4 hour drive and lots of parks and small towns close by. Fortunately the cabin was available so I reserved it and began making plans for my trip.

Reserving the cabin gave me flexibility for my stay. You never know what the weather will be like this time of year, so if it rained or snowed the entire time, I would be quite content to stay by the fireplace and spend time alone.

This is a great time to take things with you that you have put on hold for a while like reading material or a creative project. Pack the appropriate clothes for the weather or activities you want to do. Bring belongings that have special meaning or help you relax. Two key items for me were my music and my camera. Music is my passion and I listen to it all day long choosing what suits my mood of the moment. My camera is like an extra appendage for me preferring the old-fashioned style of using a manual 35mm with interchangeable lenses. When I'm in a natural setting, my eyes are constantly framing pictures of interest. If I'm lucky, some of them become good photographs.

Loving food the way I do, it is most enjoyable picking out fresh vegetables and fruit, holding them, taking in the scent and imagining what recipe would bring out the best flavor. Part of the enjoyment of this trip was preparing what I alone wanted to eat and drink; some green tea, coffee, tasty wines, fruit, cheese, vegetables, garlic and herbs and of course, chocolate. I relish all the sensations of cooking and having a kitchen in the cabin was a bonus. A delicious dinner while lounging in front of a fireplace, with a rich, bold glass of wine and music filling the air was the perfect relaxing evening.

Another bonus was the porch on the cabin. The wide porch with two rockers, table and a swing, was my favorite place to view the scenery and listen to all the surrounding sounds. I could choose to sit and meditate or venture off the porch to be a part of the nature surrounding me.

What I Learned

I learned what I've known all along. I enjoy my own company. Spending time in nature is rejuvenating, becoming one with my surroundings, reaching a state of spiritual meditation and quietness that enriches my inner self. This allows me time to balance mentally and put my life in perspective appreciating me and what I bring to others, making a difference to myself, the people I love and the world around me.

Sitting in front of the fire, the realization that my experience would be beneficial to other women became clear. It would help them to understand it's all right to spend time with yourself, away from your family, your partner and your job.

The path we walk down individually is long. We, as women, need to take the time to continue learning about ourselves. We need to get the most out of our life and discover what we find fulfilling to ourselves and those we touch along the way.

Day One

It was a cold, overcast Sunday afternoon but once on the road, a sense of freedom engulfed me and my shoulders felt lighter. Listening to Celtic music, relishing the adventure ahead, my mood became brighter. It was a straight shot heading north on I-75 and within four hours the exit approached. Instead of going straight to the cabin, there were grocery items to purchase. With the bags loaded in the back seat, I set my sights on the gravel road ahead and eased the truck to the left.

As the proprietor had mentioned, the Appalachian Museum appeared on my right. The historic site was situated on beautiful, grassy land enclosed by split rail fences comprised of old wooden buildings reminiscent of pioneer days. A white mule, some long haired oxen, goats and sheep with sweet black faces grazed or rested around the lean-to's filled with hay. A baby lamb raced across the field to its mother. Interestingly enough, to my left was a trailer park which looked odd in this landscape that took you back in time. It was time now to turn into the woods and gun the truck up the steep hill towards my destination.

The cabin came into sight first; smoke drifting out of the chimney. I stepped out of the truck and made my way up the gravel pathway to the porch. There were still small patches of snow on the ground. An old-fashioned latch opened the door to the cabin.

What a wonderful surprise! The pictures on the website did not do justice to the coziness I was feeling in the interior of the cabin. The large stone fireplace with red hot coals sent waves of heat toward me on this cold afternoon. A smile crossed my face taking in more of my surroundings. There was a quaint area to sit and enjoy eating a meal or relax with a cup of coffee or tea.

The kitchen was equipped with the all important coffee maker and a mini refrigerator. The main room had an inviting array of comfortable furniture. I could see myself curled up in the overstuffed chair with a blanket on my lap and a book in hand.

The bathroom was charming with a Victorian pedestal sink and all the comforts of home. I opened a side door and stepped out onto a tiny little porch stacked with firewood. There would be plenty of wood to keep a fire going during my stay.

I walked upstairs to the loft and though only 5' 2" tall, I still had to watch my head in the far corners of the room where the roof sloped. There was a king-sized bed filled with fluffy pillows. A table with a lamp, two chairs and a cabinet filled with extra blankets were to the left of the bed. To the right was a small willow table, floor lamp and a chest of drawers that appeared to be made out of tree limbs. There was a railing across the end of the room that looked out over the main floor.

My spirits soared. It was exactly what I was looking for to experience my first sojourn! This cabin was a place to feel comfortable in a relaxed atmosphere with no deadlines or unwanted distractions, spending my time here as I pleased.

The truck unloading began and the kitchen counter became filled with all of my special foods, wine and cooking spices. My camera bag sat in a chair by the door along with my coat, making it easy to pop outside for picture taking. I returned to the loft and placed a favorite scented candle on the small willow table. My presence had made itself known in the cabin.

Bob, the proprietor, came over to welcome me and gave me the key to the cabin and homemade breakfast for the following morning. He explained about the area and what there was to do telling me to make myself at home and to call if I needed anything. I thanked him for the wonderful fire. My evening had begun.

I opened the wooden cabinet that contained a TV, DVD's and a CD player. Soon Celtic music filled the cabin as I poured a glass of buttery Chardonnay and sang along with the music. The windows on either side of the fireplace were perfect for gazing out at the brilliant sky while preparing my dinner. One of my favorites is an array of attractively arranged hors d' Oeuvre offering a variety of tastes.

My dinner ready, I set my plate and wine glass on the hearth, grabbed a big pillow from the couch and sat on the floor in front of the fire. The spirituality of this place engulfed me, giving me a sense of purpose and tranquility, knowing I had made the right decision to make this trip.

Journal Entry One
February 18, 2007

Started my journey on my path to discovery . . .

Arrived at the cabin with a roaring fire to greet me.

My totems* hold me close. A messenger, the Hawk, sailed over my truck as I began; a heron flew to my right and horses in a trailer swiftly traveled by my side.

What a lovely place . . . the energy is wonderful.

Surrounded by the warmth of the fire and the music floating in the air.

Sojourns, Anyone?

The sun slowly sets through the trees as the first star sparkles across the sky . . . I make my wish . . . .

The Fire Dragon speaks through the fire – white hot, orange and blue flames leap upward, dancing to the Celtic music that brings life to my soul . . .

*Totems: A Totem animal is one that is with you for life, both in the physical and spiritual world. It is an animal that acts as the main guardian spirit.

~Dinner~
Sliced Fuji Apples with Roasted Red Pepper Cheese
Rosemary Breadsticks
Pumpernickel bread with Vegetable Cream Cheese
Lemon Pepper Chicken
Argentina Red Wine
Dark Chocolate Coated Cranberries for Dessert

Day Two

Awakening well-rested the next morning, I put on my warm sweater pants, topped it with a long fuzzy sweater and padded downstairs. After opening the closed wooden shutters from the night before, the bright sun lit up the cabin. My special treat for the morning was enjoying my Italian coffee with the country ham biscuit, yogurt and orange juice Bob had left the night before, while snuggling in the comfy chair and reading <u>God Winks On Love</u> by Squire Rushnell.

After bundling up for the cold, I grabbed my camera and headed out into the sunshine to take pictures. Even in the dead of winter, there was so much nature to be seen.

Birds flew all around me as I shot scene after scene.

The porch and the rocker invited me to settle in with a cup of coffee, my book and camera on the table, ready at a moment's notice.

In the early afternoon I got the urge to go out and explore the town of Norris and nearby lakes. A gallery at the end of the cabin drive looked like an interesting place to stop. It was an Appalachian gallery that housed beautiful art from people all over the state of Tennessee. From pottery to paper, glass to textiles, wood,

jewelry, copper, purses and hats, it was a marvelous place to pick up souvenirs from the area. A woman in the gallery told me about a marble statue in front of the Norris library in town.

I thanked her and headed toward the town, which was a mere crossroad in a natural setting with lovely homes and yards filled with fir trees. The marble statue was a modern take on a horn of plenty. After taking a picture, I headed back on the main road to a park by a lake. Views of open pasture land and many dairy farms passed by my window. The road led around several curves up into the mountains, finally coming to the entrance of the park tucked way back in the countryside.

The sun was starting to lower and clouds were rolling in making an interesting backdrop for the bare trees around the lake. My camera discovered some of this beauty. Driving back down the winding curves I came upon an irresistible sight and pulled the truck onto the side of the road. My camera focused on the sweetest faces of cows resting and eating on their farm.

For me, this was heaven; being able to stop when and where I wanted, to capture a memory with my camera. Bob greeted me upon my arrival back at the cabin, ready to build the fire for the evening and to leave a light breakfast for the next morning. The twilight captivated my senses sitting in the rocker on the porch with a glass of cold Chardonnay and rosemary breadsticks.

A roaring fire danced along to the music of George Winston as I cooked a delicious dinner of salmon and vegetables to savor with a glass of red wine in front of the fire. Once sated, I leaned back against the couch, took pen in hand and wrote in my journal. The words flowed easily across the page, making me realize how much I had missed capturing my thoughts on paper. A bit of an idea was forming in the back of my mind. I let go of my thoughts and gazed into the glowing embers of the fire as it died down. It would come to me in due time. Moving upstairs I lit the rain-scented candle and snuggled under the covers to read for a while, a perfect ending to my superb evening.

Journal Entry Two
February 19, 2007

What a beautiful morning! The sun peeks through the windows and once outside, the blue sky wraps around the cabin.

I sit on the porch bundled up from the cold with a steaming cup of coffee. The air is filled with song as birds glide and swirl all around me . . . brilliantly blue Bluebirds . . . winter Chickadees . . . the call of a Hawk, a Crow not far behind . . . "Thief" squawks the Blue Jay and the Carolina Wren serenades me with its sweet voice.

I venture out among the trees, ever framing pictures with my eyes . . . and then my camera.

A silent visitor appears at my feet. The imploring eyes of a golden retriever looking for a pat on the head and a belly rub.

The charm of the morning is not lost on me as I settle back down in the rocking chair watching the day unfold from the porch.

Spent the afternoon taking a drive around Norris Lake and the surrounding countryside. "Lots of cow farms. . . sweet faces."

Found a shop with local craftsmen. Beautiful work! Had a wonderful conversation with the woman there. She gave me a tour of the shop area where local craftsman can use looms, pottery wheels and a kiln. They also have a quilting rack. Found a few treasures there.

Came back and did some rocking on the porch. My dog friend promptly came by for a visit. Enjoyed a glass of wine as twilight was approaching. A young girl on horseback appeared in the yard and said "Hello" as they jumped over the split rail fence to head home.

Now I'm sitting in front of a fire with Bonnie Rait crooning and an orange sunset slowly sinking down my window framed in wood.

It has been a heavenly evening . . . good food . . . good wine . . . George Winston's piano lilting through the cabin . . . and yes . . . the fire is still going.

It has been a very spiritual evening . . .

~Dinner~
Salmon in a Butter Herb Sauce
Asparagus and Mushrooms sautéed in Butter and Garlic
Fresh Spinach Salad with Blueberries and White Balsamic Vinaigrette
Argentine Red Wine . . . again
Dark Chocolate Mango and Chili Bar and Caramel Crèmes for Dessert

Day Three

It felt good to sleep in. No noisy distractions to wake me from my night's slumber. The sky was cloudy . . . the kind of morning when you want to snuggle back under the covers and enjoy the warmth for a little longer.

Once up and moving downstairs, hunger pains led me to an enticing breakfast of quiche. Deciding to have that treat for dinner, I chose to eat brown sugar and maple oatmeal instead. I went out to the porch and made myself comfortable in the rocker with a blanket across my lap. Reading Squire's book was most intriguing and hard to put down, but nature exploring called to me. I changed clothes, prepared a snack and drove back out to the main road to Norris Dam Park.

Once on the winding road that would take me back to the park, a lovely little church appeared to my right. It was a very simple white church with stained glass windows and a most unusual steeple that housed a large bell. I closed my eyes and imagined hearing the bell ringing.

This reminded me of my grandmother's church in Kentucky. As a child, I would join my grandmother in a pew and pull out the song book. All attending would joyously sing several of the hymns, lifting our voices up to the sky. If you were lucky enough to be there during your birthday week, you got to walk up to the front and put the same amount of pennies as your birthday age into a miniature church bank. It is one of the fondest memories of my grandmother.

The road continued winding around to the entrance of the park. There were several nature paths and benches along the river and some people fishing. Much to my delight, just beyond the museum, there was an old barn and a grist mill. I decided to tour that on my way back. I drove further into the park over the bridge to the top of the dam slowly climbing up the hill to a couple of look out points. What a view from the top!

Looking out the left, there was a small marina on the lake above the dam. To the right the dam and river curved around the bottom of the hills in a peaceful, quiet setting. How it must look in the spring with the many shades of green budding out on the trees, and, in the fall, ablaze in color . . . red, orange and yellow. I took pictures and drove back over the bridge to discover more of the area around the lake.

Tucked into the hills were many restful spots to have a picnic. There were a few people taking a private hike or walking their dogs. A loop took me around the area to the foot of a hill where a trail led into the woods.

Hiking brought back memories of past adventures spent exploring the woods and the anticipation of what might be seen. I grabbed my camera and a bottle of water and stepped onto the path feeling the silence all around me. An occasional birdcall and the crunching of leaves under my feet were the only sounds heard. My camera spied a tiny bird as it rested in a tangle of branches. Even though it was serenely silent, the woods were alive with nature.

Looking down the path, I was entranced. The pale, gold leaves of the beech trees held their lacy arms out toward me on either side. It was a simple pleasure to walk past them in all their beauty. I preserved this moment with my camera. Breathing in the sweet, crisp air gave me pause to remember this smell. This smell that was as old as time; the fragrance of moss, fir and cedar trees, aging leaves and damp earth permeated the air around me. This scent reminds me of the many pleasurable hours I've spent surrounded by nature and being fulfilled and content; just happy to be. I noticed a tree to my right, its roots dug deep into the ground. The many patterns of its bark had stories to tell. One was a very human sign. It was tradition of love, a carving of two sets of initials into the trunk to hold a memory so dear. Who was E.C. and P.E. and how long ago did they pass this way?

To my left was a lone cedar tree framed by two much larger sycamore trees, their bare branches twining around the little tree or so it seemed through the lens of my camera. A memory floated back to me of a children's story about a small tree in the woods that was never chosen for a Christmas tree. But this small tree, from my viewpoint, appeared to be protected and well loved by the larger trees, giving it a space to grow between them, its evergreen branches a bright contrast to the leafless trees surrounding it.

A little further down there was a bench to sit upon and reflect. The bench was so tall my feet did not touch the ground. It made me feel like a young child again. The house where I grew up was in a wooded area with farms close by.

On many occasions, especially during the summer, I would choose a path in the woods and see where it led. One memorable adventure was exploring a trail that opened out into a meadow. I twirled around in the big, open space and ran through the tall grass down a hill. At the bottom of the hill was a small creek. Wading into the creek my hands reached under the water pulling out treasures of shiny, smooth stones. They felt good in my hand while turning them over and over looking at the colors of cream, brown and black made glossy by the wetness.

I stuffed my pockets with the stones and sat back on the bank. The creek gurgled as it wound around the edge of the woods. It was a soothing sound and I closed my eyes to listen.

It was one of those wonderful moments when you realize you have found the most special place to be your own secret hideaway. A place you can go when you want to be alone and imagine the extraordinary.

The vivid memory faded, but sitting so peacefully on the bench, I could recapture that moment in time and feel much the same as I did those years ago. I looked out through the trees into the bluegreen water of the lake and listened as the waves gently rolled up against the shore. This would be another memory to recall when I needed to block out the noises of everyday life for a respite of solitude.

Taking a lower path back towards the beginning of the trail brought me to a most unusually shaped tree. It was like a sculptor had carved shapes into the limbs. I observed the tree for several minutes as if it were a painting in a museum, seeing something different from each angle.

My first thought was that of a graceful antelope leaping through the center of the tree where the branches met the trunk. There were many raised knots and holes in the branches, twisting around the trunk at odd angles. The limbs were thick and then thinned out randomly only to thicken again.

I took a picture of the tree to study its shapes again and again.

A little further down was a delightful tree, bent sideways and leaning out over the water. Someone had nailed long narrow strips of wood from the base out onto the widest part of a limb. It was a perfect perch to climb up to and dangle your feet out over the water. I thought of the swimming hole my mother had often told me about. During the summer months she, her brother and cousins would climb up a cherry tree and swing out over the water, jumping at the last possible moment making a huge splash as they landed, laughter and squeals abounding.

My steps took me back to the truck. This hike turned out to be one of the most spiritual moments of my sojourn. It held all of the elements of rejuvenation for me. I was surrounded by quiet beauty that had been untouched for centuries. I looked up in awe at the tall trees surrounding me as they danced gently in the breeze. What were the whispers of wisdom they imparted? The moments spent in the woods were inspiring and helped me to focus on my inner self.

My exploration took me back to the museum. The building appeared to be closed but there was a path around the back that led to the grist mill. It was a working mill but not open during the winter. The base of the mill was stacked stone and the upper part was weathered timber with the old paddle wheel on the side. I could picture the water dripping from shelf to shelf as the wheel went round and round grinding the corn into meal. The song "John Barleycorn" wandered through my mind.

The woods surrounding the mill were very old with moss-covered trees twisting their roots above the ground in intricate knots. A bubbling stream ran alongside with miniature waterfalls spilling through the rocks and water pooling at the bottom, clear as glass. Across the way was an old barn. A large blue wagon rested under the eaves on the side of the barn. It wasn't hard to imagine a mule hooked up to the wagon pulling in loads of corn to be ground at the mill. It was a reminder of an era long past, when life was simple and we respected the land as we took from nature what it would give to us. My camera shutter clicked saving these bygone images. The day at the park left me feeling very peaceful and content.

I decided to drive into the town of Clinton to check out the shops. Inside the rock shop on the corner was every kind of stone imaginable. When I was a teenager, my mom had a simple, dark green jade ring. I've always liked jade and my favorite color is green. Mom's ring looked very attractive on my hand and she allowed me to wear it. The smoothness of the jade felt good on my finger. Mom gave it to me and I wore it for many years. Much later, I discovered the properties of jade were practicality, wisdom, mental peace and tolerance of others. I sorted through the polished stone rings and selected colors that reflected my daughters' personalities hoping they too would get as much enjoyment out of wearing their rings.

The antique shops were filled to bursting making it an adventure to search through them. There were many beautiful pieces of furniture, glassware, collectibles and jewelry.

Funny how looking at an object of the past can evoke so many memories, bringing them to life as if it were only yesterday. I am very sentimental and that is why my vintage possessions are so special to me. My collection of vintage clothing and accessories began as a young girl. There is something so intriguing about owning things that are from another era and making them uniquely yours. When I wear a vintage dress it's fun to imagine what the previous owner was like. Was this her favorite dress? Did she wear a hat and matching jewelry with it?

A portion of my jewelry collection consists of rhinestone clips in assorted shapes and sizes with clear or colored crystals. Wearing them with any style of clothing adds a sense of glamour and mystique to my persona. My Great Aunt Marie's husband owned a nightclub in the 40's and she had beautiful costume jewelry, purses and hats. When she died, her jewelry was passed on to my family. My sisters and I were allowed to pick out a couple of pieces for ourselves. I chose a pair of beautiful triangular clips set with periwinkle blue and clear rhinestones.

My favorite vintage accessory from my Great Aunt is an authentic leopard fur hat. She had a group of friends that were very close and one of these women owned a full length leopard fur coat. In her will, the woman left the coat to her friends who chose to cut the coat up and design their own keepsakes. My Great Aunt had a belt and a pillbox hat made. A favorite picture of my daughter Kelsey is in her diaper standing in her youth bed adorned with black cat eye sunglasses and Great Aunt Marie's leopard fur hat! I cherish my vintage collection and will gradually pass pieces on to my daughters so they can share their histories with the next generation.

I finally drove back to the cabin to enjoy one more sunset from the porch and one more dinner by the fire. The night was filled with large claps of thunder and lightning that lit up the cabin, waking me several times during the night. I dozed back to sleep, happy to be warm and dry in a comfortable bed.

Journal Entry Three
February 20, 2007

Started my morning with spiritual Celtic music. Bundled up and sat out on the porch to read. A steaming hot cup of coffee and a blanket gave warmth on this gray, overcast day.

The dogs joined me on the porch and after some affection, they settled down and slept while I read. A Hawk flew around the property, its cry piercing the air as if to say, "I am here for you".

Had a very peaceful day in nature. Explored the Norris Dam Park. Took lots of pictures and did some hiking. How spiritual it was to sit among the trees gazing out at the green/blue water of the lake as the waves gently lapped up on the shore. Some Canadian Geese broke the silence as they winged across the lake on their journey.

Checked out the antique stores in the town of Clinton. Then, back to the porch to enjoy night coming on with a glass of wine. My dog companions joined me. They have become my protectors. Spoke with both of the proprietors having a lively conversation about teenagers and surviving them.

Had a phone conversation on the porch with Kim, my sister, relaying to her the wonderfulness of this place.

Now I sit in front of the fire . . . Spanish guitar fills the soul of this cabin . . . such passion! Thanks Dawn for the wonderful CD!

~Dinner~
Cheese and Broccoli Quiche
Asparagus and Mushroom Sauté
Carrot and Pineapple Muffin
Delicious Red Wine from Chile
Dark Chocolate Covered Ginger for Dessert

Day Four

My last morning was spent on the porch watching nature come to life after the storm. It was in this special place that thoughts previously forming in the back of my mind finally came forth. These few days had been a very profound experience for me. I would write a book about my sojourn to encourage other women to take sojourns of their own.

We all have many phases we go through in life. You start out young thinking anything is possible and little by little reality creeps in. Lessons are taught to us and some are learned. Your life becomes molded by the people and surroundings in it. They are a part of how you become you. As we grow, our experiences are carefree when young, very intense in the acutely aware teenage years, and then heightened with passion for life as we become young adults moving out into the world to make a place for ourselves. At that point, responsibility is knocking at the door and if you accept, your life is forever changed. The pace becomes so extreme over the years that we risk leaving our true selves behind to grow into what we vaguely want to be or think we should be.

My trip made me realize that what I wanted at this time in my life was to have myself back. There had to be a way to balance the old me with the discoveries revealed in my life thus far. I had kissed my way through the proverbial lineup of frogs and found my prince to marry.

Taking my time before jumping into motherhood, once pregnant I asked myself, "Will I still be me or will I change?" I became a mother and lost me. Raising my children has been my most fulfilling and loving legacy, but bit by bit, family needs took over leaving less and less time for me. As a wife and a mom you have to make choices that forever shape your life. My choices made me happy but I became complacent. A part of me was missing and I wanted it back.

I opened my mind and shut down the noise in my brain during my stay at the cabin. Listening to my inner voice and taking deep breaths helped me to mentally calm myself. Physically releasing stress opened me up to enjoy the simplicity of the moment. The pleasure and passion of life began to return to me. Positive energy began flowing through my body. My spiritual self was returning and I embraced it. My energies had been disbursed through a blur of continuous motion. It was time to take responsibility for myself again; to get back to nurturing my soul and focusing this positive energy into all aspects of my daily life.

The time had come to go. My stay was recorded in the guest book for the Cabin on Cedar Ridge promising to recommend this wonderful place to those who would enjoy it. Packed and ready to go I stood in the driveway looking around, taking in all the special moments of this trip.

The day was absolutely gorgeous. The air was warm for February and once on the road, I rolled the windows down and with the wind blowing through my hair, sang at the top of my lungs as one familiar song after another played on the radio. I had not felt this free in a long time, refreshed and energized, ready to take on whatever came across my path. I was confident that all my worries and frustrations would seem less insurmountable and balancing my life would be easier. Now I'm wondering what took me so long to take a sojourn with myself!

Sojourns, Anyone?

Journal Entry Four
February 21, 2007

Had quite a thunder storm last night which has continued on to this morning. It's interesting to imagine what that would have been like in 1860, the era this cabin was built.

Mother Nature opening up the heavens, the sharp crack of thunder and bright streaks of lightning bouncing across the dark, night sky . . .

Now the rain falls . . . a comforting sound. In the daylight everything glistens and is new all over again. A squirrel jumps across the split rail fence and the birds sing good morning. A light breeze brushes across my face as I swing on the porch, my dear dog friend at my feet.

Sojourns, Anyone?

These are the days to cherish . . . these moments of solitude . . . once I'm back on the fast track I call my daily life. When my days reach that never ending hectic pitch . . . this is what I'll remember . . . I'll take that five minutes . . . back in time to sit on the porch while nature took its course.

Why Take a Sojourn?

Women need to take a break from their routine, spend some time getting grounded and discover themselves all over again. A sojourn is making time for doing what only you want to do with no responsibilities attached. Simply be of the moment. You can use the following checklists to help guide you on your own journey.

- Take time to go to a quiet place where there are no distractions.
- Meditate.
- Renew your spiritual self.
- Get back in touch with nature; feel the energy coming from the earth.
- Spend time with your creative side.
- Simply spend time doing what you love to do, whether it's reading, listening to music, sleeping, eating your favorite foods, painting or some other passion.

Sojourns, Anyone?

When you make the decision to take a trip, spend some time thinking about what you want to get out of your experience.

- Do you want to go somewhere that is very quiet and full of solitude?
- Do you want to get closer to nature?
- Do you want to go somewhere and be pampered?
- Do you want an adventure, to try something you've never done before?
- Do you want to do something you once did a long time ago and really enjoyed?
- Do you want to be by the water, the desert, the mountains?
- Do you want to be somewhere exotic or someplace close to home?

The wonderful thing about a sojourn is there are no set times or deadlines. Be flexible and be spontaneous; do whatever moves you or feels right at the moment. These are memories you are making that will sustain you until you take your next trip. The next step is to get a mind-set that you ARE going to take this journey. Pick a date and think about where you want to go.

Your Sojourn....

Think about a location you would like to visit and determine the distance you are willing to travel. Start thinking about lodging and what is important to you about the facilities and the surrounding area.

How do you want to travel?
- by car
- by boat or ship
- by train
- by plane
- horseback

Where do you want to stay?
- hotel
- Airbnb or bed and breakfast (B&B)
- resort
- cabin
- condo
- camping/RV
- hostel

What type of amenities do you want?
- someplace with a kitchen or just a mini refrigerator
- someone to prepare meals for you
- hot tub or whirlpool bath

Sojourns, Anyone?

- if camping, electricity and running water
- a fireplace
- luxurious linens
- a pool
- a spa
- 5-Star restaurant
- maid service
- beautiful grounds/gardens
- simple room
- room with a view

What do you want to have close?
- beach
- lake
- woods
- parks
- hiking/walking trails
- gardens
- historical sites
- quaint towns and shops
- antique shopping
- spa
- seasonal activities
- mountains
- boat access
- unusual restaurants
- museums
- galleries

- bird/wildlife sanctuary
- music events
- literature events
- sporting activities

Now it's time to start researching to plan your sojourn.

Ways to Research Your Sojourn:
- internet
- travel books
- newspapers/magazines
- AAA
- chamber of commerce/city hall
- family and friends
- word of mouth
- travel channel
- board of tourism
- travel agent
- past trips

The Internet

Using the internet puts ample amounts of information right at your fingertips, which can be overwhelming. Narrow down your search when you first start researching.

Try picking the area you are interested in traveling to, then query places to stay, like hotels, Airbnb, VRBO or B&B's. Another suggestion would be to pick a state or country and then select a city or town. Once you are on the site, there will be all kinds of links for lodging, events, things to do in the area, restaurants, etc. You would be amazed how much information you can find even about a small town in the middle of nowhere. You can almost always get some basic information.

Airbnb and VRBO have their own websites. Many states have certified B&B sites. The proprietors have certain guidelines of quality they have to follow to be a part of these associations.

National and State Parks have very informative websites with reasonably priced lodging. These are great places to stay if you want to be surrounded by nature.

All of the hotel chains have websites that will easily link you to their hotels in the area you've chosen to travel to. They also have extended links for things to do in the area.

Travel Books
    Travel books, although they may seem old fashioned compared to the internet, still offer a unique way to get travel information. Most books have up-to-date information and cover very high-end to budget

traveling. You can also find very interesting information about out of the way places.

Going to a bookstore can be very enjoyable, sitting down with a cup of coffee or tea and doing research on a trip. The atmosphere is great and gives you a sense of excitement about what you may discover on your trip.

Newspapers and Magazines

Newspapers and magazines have articles on unusual places to go and give ways to get more detailed information if you have an interest. Many memorable trips can be taken to places you might never have known about had it not been for an article that caught your eye.

AAA

An annual membership to AAA is minimal and an excellent idea for a woman traveling by herself. With the membership, you get road service, 10 – 20% discounts on approved AAA hotels, restaurants and attractions, maps, tour books and trip tickets which map your route and point out places to stop along the way.

No Planning

Again, not everyone likes to plan. Not planning can make for an exciting and memorable sojourn. Just choose your mode of transportation and go where your path leads you.

Chamber of Commerce and City Halls

A local Chamber of Commerce or City Hall is a great way to get firsthand information on where you've chosen to travel to as well as the surrounding area. You can either go to their website or contact them by phone.

Family and Friends

Family and friends can be very helpful. Someone you know may own a second home or know of someone that does. They may have information on places they've vacationed.

Word of Mouth

The same thing can be said for word of mouth. Co-workers, people you meet at a party or gathering, striking up a conversation with the person next to you, even standing in line waiting for a service could lead to a place to take your sojourn.

Travel Channel

Who doesn't enjoy being an armchair traveler? Take it to the next level and actually go to someplace you've seen on TV.

Board of Tourism

The Board of Tourism is chock-full of information. They will send you free brochures, maps and other information about the area you want to travel to. They also have excellent websites with many links.

Travel Agent

If you don't have the time or don't care to do your own research, contact a travel agent. Give them an idea of where you want to go, what your budget is and what interests you have and let them do the research for you. They can plan your trip and all you have to do is pick up the itinerary and go. There may be a service charge to use a travel agent.

Past Trips

Maybe you have the memory of a favorite vacation; an area or place that you really enjoyed and would like to go back to. Sometimes going someplace familiar is comfortable yet you can experience new things there.

Sojourns, Anyone?

Once you've done your research, begin making any arrangements you need to prepare in advance such as lodging reservations or events you want to attend. Just keep an open mind about your trip and everything else will fall into place.

I'm sharing my experience with you to let you get a sense of what it is like to break out of the mold and focus on yourself. This book gives you the tools to begin creating your own journey of re-discovery and to gain a sense of balance in your existing world.

Have fun getting to know yourself all over again!

Safe Journeys,

Kathy

Kathy

* I would love to hear from you and talk about your sojourn. You can contact me at kathy@fernheadpublishing.com or on Instagram @kattyrat18.

Food For Thought

Because food was an important part of my sojourn, I want to share some of my thoughts and recipes with you.

Hors d'oeuvres

There's something very special about enjoying a quiet sunset from a porch. A simple feast is in order while watching the sun sink below the horizon.

Combinations of salty, sweet, crunchy and soft foods are tasty for a moment such as this.

Hors d'oeuvre Plate
- Juicy orange sections
- Crunchy rosemary breadsticks
- A favorite cheese or cheese spread
- Bruschetta
- Thin slices of chicken with sun dried tomatoes
- Ripe strawberries
- Hummus with apple slices or grapes
- Salted or smoked almonds
- Smoked salmon with a bit of capers and dill

Put together any bite full of your favorite finger food along with a lush creamy Chardonnay, a tart Sauvignon Blanc, a light Pinot Noir, a fruit drink or a cup of tea.

Enjoy one of life's simple pleasures in your own company.

Chicken

Sometimes the occasion calls for a meal that will sustain you more; especially if you've worked up an appetite enjoying your favorite activity during the day.

This is my favorite chicken recipe. It is quick and easy and the chicken is always very flavorful and moist.

Some of the seasonings you might want to try:
- Fresh minced or dried herbs
- Cajun seasoning
- Lemon pepper
- Dijon or cranberry mustard
- Mediterranean seasoning or any other favorite seasoning blend.

There are many delicious varieties available now in groceries or specialty stores. You can also make your own by blending together some spices with salt and pepper, adding a little bit of olive oil to make a paste, then spread onto the chicken.

Pre-heat the oven to 400° F

Ingredients
1 – 4 chicken breast
Olive oil
Salt, pepper and seasonings

Flatten your chicken breast, if needed, with a meat mallet to ¼ inch thickness. Cover both sides of the chicken with a seasoned paste or flavored mustard. If you are using a dry seasoning, brush some olive oil on the chicken, sprinkle with the seasoning, salt and pepper (optional) turn the chicken breast over and repeat. Bake in the oven for 12 minutes or until the juices run clear.

The chicken breast can be eaten whole or sliced into strips or chunks to go into salads, as pizza toppings, serve on a cracker or add to a slice of sundried tomato. Use your imagination!

Roasted Vegetables

There is nothing better than fresh vegetables! One of the most flavorful ways to cook vegetables is to roast them. A little bit of olive oil, salt and pepper is all you need to enhance the natural flavor of your favorite vegetable.

Vegetables that are good roasted:
Asparagus   Cauliflower
Green beans   Assorted colors of bell peppers
Carrots   Turnips and parsnips

General Instructions
Pre-heat oven to 425° F

Wash vegetables and dry off (blot with paper towels). Put vegetables on a cookie sheet. Sprinkle with olive oil, salt and pepper. Stir vegetables until well coated and spread out flat. Put pan in oven and stir every 5 minutes until done. Vegetables should be tender and a bit blackened.

Variations

- Asparagus: To prepare, snap the bottom tough end off the stalk. Cook at 425° for 15 minutes.
- Green Beans: To prepare, leave beans whole or snap in half for smaller pieces. Cook at 425° F for 15 minutes.
- Carrots: Peel and slice ¼ inch or use pre washed baby carrots. Cook at 425° F for 15 – 25 minutes.
- Cauliflower: Cut head into florets. Cook at 450° F for 15 – 25 minutes.
- Turnips and parsnips: Peel and slice ¼ inch. If large slices, you can cut in half or quarter. Cook at 425° F for 20 – 25 minutes.
- Assorted colored bell peppers: Slice into strips. Cut strips in half for smaller pieces. Cook at 425° F for 15 – 20 minutes.

Seasoning Variations
- After vegetables are done cooking, sprinkle with freshly grated Parmesan or Romano cheese.
- Carrots: Before putting carrots on cookie sheet, put in bowl. For 1 lb of carrots, melt 1 or 2 TB of butter and pour over carrots, sprinkle with Cajun seasoning and squeeze some honey to taste over carrots. Mix together in bowl; spread carrots flat on cookie sheet.
- Cauliflower and turnips: Sprinkle herbs or mixed seasoning on vegetables along with salt, pepper and oil. Stir to coat.
- Parsnips: Squeeze some honey over vegetables after sprinkling with salt and pepper and stir to coat.

Vegetables are that extra something that keeps a meal balanced. Be adventuresome and try new tastes to enhance the richness of your food!

Salads

A salad is such a versatile meal. It can be eaten as an entrée, a side dish or a mere garnish on a plate.

We are fortunate to have so many choices of salad greens. Varieties include iceberg, romaine, red leaf, boston, spinach, mixed field greens and herbs. You can buy fresh salad greens or many choices of bagged salad greens and herbs.

Today, food preparation is even more convenient with traditional additions, such as vegetables added to salad, already washed and precut. You can purchase sliced or julienne carrots, prewashed, sliced mushrooms and cauliflower or broccoli florets. The grocery stores have chopped or sliced vegetables available fresh on a daily basis. Fresh cut fruit is available in small to large serving size containers. Dried fruit of all kinds is also available.

Many varieties of cheeses are available preshredded, crumbled or in chunks to add to a salad. You can also purchase blocks of cheese and shred your own.

To add crunchiness to a salad, you can throw in any kind of nut, sesame sticks, croutons or crumbled bacon.

My favorite salad green is spinach. Here is a
delicious, simple salad to make:
- Fresh spinach leaves (either pre-washed or
wash off yourself)
- Fresh blueberries washed off - Gorgonzola
cheese crumbles
- Fresh sliced mushrooms
- Pine nuts

Put spinach in a bowl and add other ingredients; pour
dressing over salad and add some freshly ground
pepper.

Salad Dressings

For a simple salad dressing, pour a small amount
of balsamic vinegar in a bowl, add a small amount of
extra virgin olive oil and whisk together. You can add
more olive oil depending on how thick you want your
dressing to be.
You can add variations to your salad dressing:
- Sprinkle in some herbs
- Dijon mustard or any other flavored
mustard
- Salt and pepper
- Pinch of sugar
- Minced garlic or onion
- Orange, lime or lemon juice
- Try other flavored vinegars or oils

For an entrée salad add:
- Chicken
- Salmon
- Turkey - Shrimp
- Steak
- Pork
- Garbanzo Beans
- Black Beans
- Corn or Corn relish

Simply said, add your favorite ingredients to any type of greens and you have made the perfect salad for you!

Chocolate

A taste of chocolate is enough to make anyone feel special. One bite delivers so much pleasure it's an experience in itself!

What do you think of when you hear the word chocolate?

- Chocolate truffles
- Dark chocolate
- Chocolate-covered nuts
- Chocolate fudge
- Chocolate ice cream
- Milk chocolate
- Chocolate covered cherries
- Candy coated chocolate pieces
- White chocolate
- Hot chocolate
- Chocolate kisses
- Bittersweet chocolate
- Chocolate ganache
- Chocolate milkshake
- Triple-layer chocolate cake
- Chocolate brownies

Everyone has their favorite chocolate. Sometimes it's just a taste or sometimes it's an entire dessert.

My first love was milk chocolate, loving every creamy bite. Then I had my first taste of dark chocolate covered ginger. The intricacies of the flavors were amazing. I ventured even further into the world of dark chocolate and have become a huge fan. It is especially good with a glass of full bodied Merlot. Chocolate is an exceptional way to end a meal.

Go to gourmet shops or food stores that carry gourmet items. There are many choices of candy and chocolate desserts. Experiment and try your favorite chocolate with a new twist like a milk chocolate bar with orange peel, a white chocolate bar with bits of dried cranberry or a dark chocolate bar with red chili peppers. Try coffee ice cream with ribbons of chocolate fudge running through it. A chocolate cake layered with chocolate ganache and raspberries, mint chocolate chip brownies or chocolate bread pudding.

The choices are endless. No matter what you choose, it is that special touch to make your evening memorable.

About The Author

Inspired by spiritual connections gained through her travels to different landscapes, people and their cultures, Kathy Meenach shares her experiences with women across the country and encourages them to take a sojourn of their own.

Where to find Sojourns, Anyone?
www.fernheadpublishing.com
(paperback, digital eBook)
www.amazon.com (paperback, kindle)

Where to find Kathy
Instagram @kattyrat18
kathy@fernheadpublishing.com

CPSIA information can be obtained
at www.ICGtesting.com
Printed in the USA
LVHW031434030521
686343LV00012B/131

9 780998 219936